MORPHÊ

MRGD

 Springer Wien New York

RIEA.ch Concept Series
General Editor: Lebbeus Woods

MRGD
MORPHÊ

c/o RIEA (Research Institute for Experimental Architecture)
Bern, Switzerland, Europe

© 2008 Springer-Verlag/Wien and RIEA Europa
Printed in Austria

SpringerWienNewYork is a part of
Springer Science & Business Media
springer.at

Printing: Holzhausen Druck & Medien GmbH, 1140 Wien

Printed on acid-free and chlorine-free bleached paper
With numerous illustrations

SPIN: 12174379
Library of Congress Control Number: 2008923575

ISSN 1610-0719
ISBN 978-3-211-75789-5 SpringerWienNewYork

General Editor
Lebbeus Woods

3D-Renderings, Models and Photography by
MRGD

Graphic Design
H1reber, büro destruct, Bern, 2008

CONTENT

PREFACE

Autopoietic Elegance
Patrik Schumacher

Morphê is one of those rare design research projects where a radically process driven design research culminates in an extraordinary elegance. The elegance instantiated here thrives on complexity rather than simplicity. The sense of elegance indicates that an intricate problem has been beautifully resolved. Elegance articulates complexity.

The complexity is initially produced from within a closed computational system, the Maya hair dynamic system. Here arrays of lines are manipulated by means of mutual attraction (cling) forces while simultaneously responding to quasi-gravitational forces. The system is able to dynamically resolve any initial geometry together with any configuration of forces by producing resultant configurations that display both the rich differentiation and the lawful coherency that we would expect in complex natural systems. This internal regime of producing ordered complexity can be utilized to absorb, process and articulate external complexity as long as we are able to represent this complexity within the system. For instance, the multiple directions by which paths hit or dissect a site might be taken as the initial set up for the dynamical system.

The project does indeed initially proceed from planar path-systems. It then moves on to explore three-dimensional webs, and then tries to look for coincidences between paths-ways and structural logics. The quasi-physics of the hair-system is being paralleled by the exploration of the real physics and material logic of webs made from curving steel wires. Then surfaces are introduced to generate platforms for accommodation as well as producing a tight fitting enclosing envelope. This envelope surface – which filters the internal complexity without obliterating it - is then populated by generative components that are sensitive and responsive to the subtle differentiations that are embedded within these surfaces. The components translate the differences in orientation and curvature into a differential component morphology. The ability to set up such chains of lawful correlation turns the designer from a form-giver into a law-maker. In the case of Morphê path-systems are traced by structural logics, which in turn are filtered by a surface-curvature logic, which in turn is finally accentuated by a responsive component morphology. Then light plays upon this deep relief as yet another layer of parametric translation.

The way these various systems feed into each other follows the paradigm of autopoeisis rather than the paradigm of mechanical translation. The difference is perhaps best exemplified by the difference between kicking a ball and kicking a dog. The first case is a rigid cause and effect connection, the second is a stimulus – response mechanism whereby the response is highly mediated via selective cognition and internal processing of the stimulus. Instead of simply being pervaded and fully determined by an exterior impulse, autopoeitic systems maintain an arsenal of response options that can be selected and combined according to internal logics that evolve on the basis of experiences. Instead of a cause-and-effect model we might use a stimulus-response model, or even better a cognition-information-processing model. The cognition and information processing of autopoeitic systems depends as much on its internal state as on its external environment. The way the various computational subsystems of the associative parametric model are sensitive to each other is best analysed in analogy to autopoeitic systems. Just like a series of structurally coupled autopeitic systems the different layers of the associative-parametric model each encompass a whole range of response options that the designer can calibrate. Each layer is an autopeitic system and simultaneously a subsystem in an encompassing autopeitic system. No linear point to point correlations need to be assumed from layer to layer. The designer can script associative functions that entail inverse relations, thresholds and turning points. The system's overall operating laws can be made sensitive to the urban context. Contextual nuances can then ripple through the system in a generative cascade that can be invented and calibrated by the designer.

It is this sense of autopoeitic complexity that assimilates this work to organic natural systems, where all forms are the result of intricately interacting selections. Just like natural systems, elegant compositions are so highly integrated that they cannot be neatly decomposed – a major point of difference in comparison with the modern design paradigm of clear separation of functional subsystems. Instead of the separation of subsystems we emphasize the structural coupling or organic inter-articulation of subsystems.

The exploitation of natural morphologies as a source domain for analogical transference into architecture made a substantial contribution to the development of a new fluid language of architecture. This new architectural language is marked by a new level of intricate coherency in the deployment of curvilinear geometry that can articulate complex arrangements and relationships without losing out on legibility and the capacity to orient users.

With Morphê we go further: from imitating nature to the creation of a second nature – with an enormous gain in freedom of creation. We are moving from a new architectural language to a whole new paradigm for architecture.

It was Frei Otto who most systematically harnessed the lawfulness of physical systems as form-finding procedure to generate his design-morphology. The results have been striking. Morphê is taking Frei Otto's work as one of its major sources of inspiration. Lars Spuybroek has described these form-finding processes as "material computing". Such analog form-finding processes can complement the new digital design tools. The new digital tools might in fact be best described as quasi-physical form-finding processes. The most advanced tools – like Generative Components – offer associative logics that allow the designer to set up complex systems of parametric interaction. Any parameter of any object might be dynamically correlated with any parameter of any other object within the model. This means that the designer might craft an artificial "universe", with its own peculiar "ontology" and "laws of nature". The formal/spatial systems that can be generated now start to look more and more like natural systems where all modulations are the result of the complex interaction of physical forces or like organic system where the forms result from a similar play of forces selected from a much wider range and integrated in adaptation to diverse performance requirements.

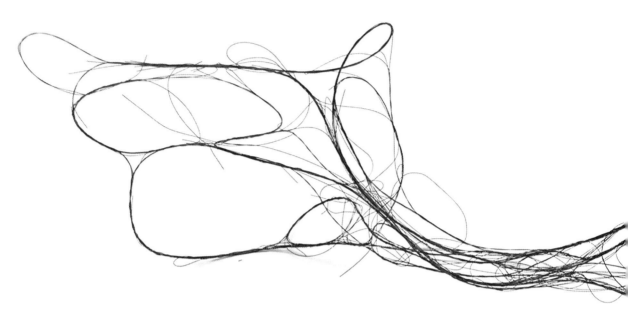

A specific aspect of this overall lawful and integrated nature of elegance is the capacity of elegant "compositions" to adapt to complex urban contexts. Adaptive capacity or adaptation is another key ambition of the contemporary avant-garde trend that might suggest comparison with natural organic systems. An architectural system that has an enhanced capacity to adapt to its environment will result in an intricate artifact-context ensemble that has sublated initial contradictions into a new complex synthesis that further enhances the overall sense of sophisticated elegance. The model for adaptation here is again based on the concept of autopoeisis - with a principally unlimited range of possible contextual affiliations – rather than assuming straightforward assimilation. Autopoeitic affiliation is inherently unpredictable. But you recognize it when you see it. There is a strong sense of fitness and correspondence – without always being able to realize how this is being achieved.

This capacity for unexpected, "magical" forms of contextual adaptation has been powerfully demonstrated by Morphê. The way this new multi-layered construct affiliates and symbiotically fuses with Centre Point tower is rather striking. The talented eye remains a crucial arbiter in the steering of the associative set up towards a visually effective articulation of complexity. In architecture we ultimately care only about those intricacies that can be experienced.

Morphê is demonstrating how the strategic harnessing of the new computational power can lead to a new style in the best sense of the word. A new style in this sense has two critical aspects: A new style coheres a research programme that proceeds from a unique paradigm determining the paradigmatic problems, preferred methods and evaluative criteria of avant-garde design research. A new style is also unique with respect to its phenomenology, i.e. its visual appearance and articulatory power to orient the relevant life processes; unique in what it demands from us in terms of attentional focus and perceptive comprehension. Morphê participates in the formation of a new style in this sense. The paradigmatic problematic of this new style is the design of associative logics and its phenomenological agenda is autopeitic elegance. This style is well under way and is building up towards a hegemonic position within the avant-garde of architecture. But it has not been christened yet. My proposal is to call it Parametricism. For me Morphê gives us a compelling instance of this new style.

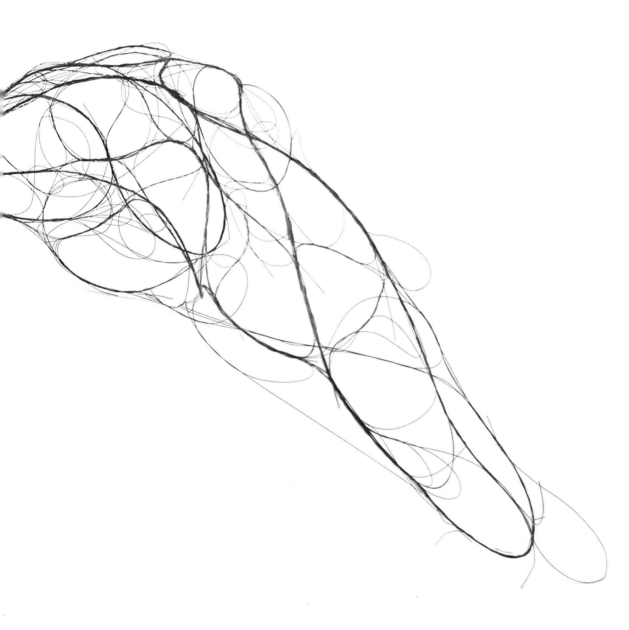

INTRODUCTION

Serious Play: Operational Hairs
Theodore Spyropoulos

*"Play and learning are intimately intertwined, and it is not too difficult
to demonstrate a relationship between intelligence and play."*
Marshall McLuhan, (1965)

In September 1969, a landmark issue of Architectural Design guest edited by Roy Landau brought issues of interaction and digital computation to mainstream architectural media. The issue featured articles by Nicholas Negroponte, Cedric Price, Warren Brodey, and the cybernetician Gordon Pask. Pask in his article The Architectural Relevance of Cybernetics argued that *"architects are first and foremost system designers who have been forced to take an increasing interest in the organizational system properties of development, communication and control"* (Pask, 1969). He argued that architecture had no theory to cope with the pressing contemporary complexities of the time and only through a cybernetic understanding of systemic processes could the architect evolve his practice.

A year later Nicholas Negroponte, then director of the MIT's Architecture Machine Group, professed that we find ourselves in, *"a day of evolutionary revolution... let us build machines that can learn, can grope, and can fumble, machines that will be architectural partners, architectural machines"* (Negroponte, 1970). Many of the initial discussions in the late sixties underlying adaptive and evolutionary models of design and computation have recently resurfaced as contemporary design and production processes have embraced digital design methods. What was primarily discursive in that period has transformed as the information revolution has given rise to new forms of design practice.

The work of MRGD developed at the Architectural Association's Design Research Lab speculates on this potential through playful misuse of Maya hair dynamics and exhaustive examination of the inherent generative spatial organizations as a product of their interplay. Material based prototypes and associative design systems serve as conversational feedback mechanisms that set to define the advanced forms of integration necessary to deploy hair as a spatial structuring instrument. It is through this catalog of possibilities that MRGD achieves a body of research that is generative, creative and truly affords the potential for varied and unexpected outcomes. This reminds us of what John Frazer highlighted in his seminal book An Evolutionary Architecture on the subject of digital design tools that *"perhaps... the real benefits are found in having to rethink explicitly and clearly the way in which we habitually do things."* (Frazer 1995)

Bibliography:
Frazer, John. (1995) An Evolutionary Architecture. London: Architectural Association Publications.
Negroponte, Nicholas. (1970) The Architecture Machine: Toward a More Human Environment: Cambridge, MA / London: MIT Press.
Pask, Gordon. (1969), "The Architectural Relevance of Cybernetics", Architectural Design, September, pp. 494–6.

PROJECT BRIEF

According to Christopher Alexander, compartmentalization and the dissociation of internal elements are potential signs of anarchy and schizophrenia. He argues for an understanding of our environment as a complex interconnected field of overlapping boundaries rather than one divided into crisp sets and subsets.

MRGD looked into fuzzy logic, a theory dealing with reasoning that is approximate rather than precisely deduced from classical predicate logic. It argues that as complexity rises, precise statements lose meaning and meaningful statements lose precision. MRGD examined the potential of fuzzy logic as a loose-fit organizational technique for developing intelligent, flexible and adaptive environments.

The featured project Urban Lobby is MRGD's attempt to explore the potentiality of some of the conclusions of this research against an existing urban context. Seeing the project as a testing ground for its computational tools and design techniques, the studio expanded its research territory from focusing and systemizing the dynamic hair tool as a generative design machine to a larger scale, involving levels of social, cultural and global organizations. Urban Lobby also explored ways of producing architectural interventions based on an understanding of the city as a field of dynamics. The primary focus was to create an impact on the selected confined site and its immediate adjacencies by making infrastructure develop into architecture.

The Urban Lobby is thought to be a continually contested and negotiated transient space, a public living room, a private boardroom, an orientation space, a public and private open space, a subway business lounge, etc. The resultant possibility of 'lobbying' is an investigation rooted in creative and critical speculations on how one addresses contemporary modes of urbanity and interfacing. Currently, Center Point, an iconic 70s high-rise building in the centre of London, is comprised of a number of scattered subway entries that link through tangled labyrinths to the subway lines. In addition, the density of the urban commercial and retail fabric provides generative architectural opportunities as well as direct resistance for growth and connectivity. The high level of pedestrian activity of the area and the convergence of millions of commuters at its current transportation hub provide the site with an intricate connectivity problem.The project carries the ideas of blurred boundaries, interplay and interaction into the building's interior; different lobbies will be plugged in and distributed along the office building's facade: a scheme that will replace the earlier concept of Atrium and whose primary role is to speed vertical circulation and communication, establishing interim gathering places throughout the building.

SPECULATIVE EXPERIMENTATION

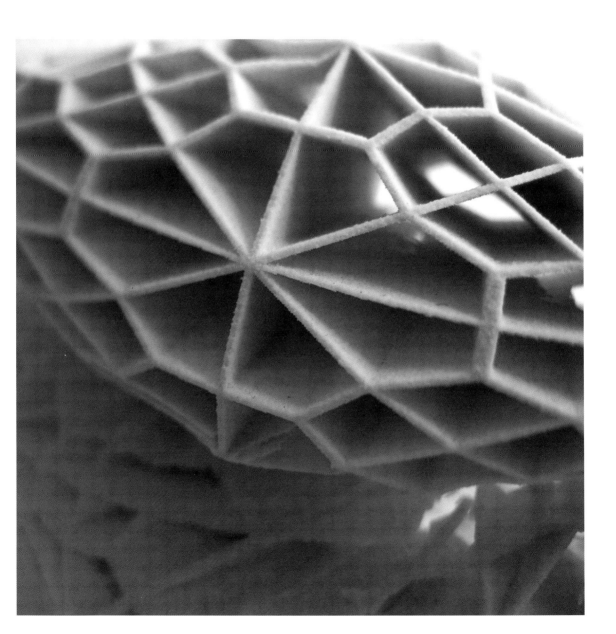

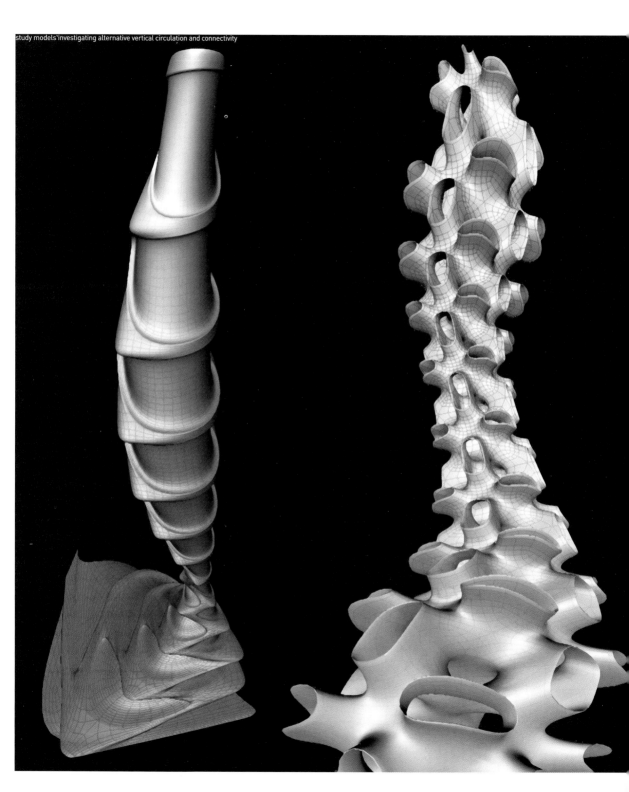

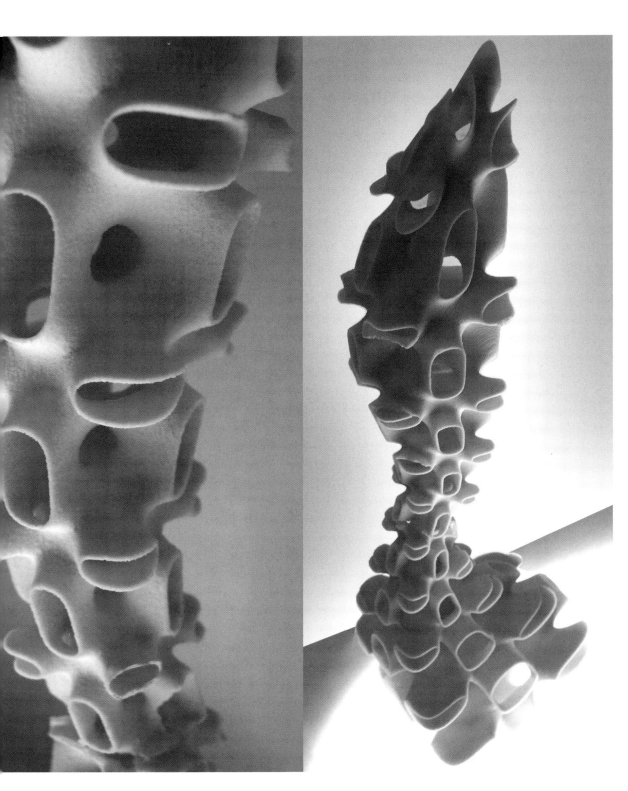

FIELD CONDITIONS

These experiments aim to demonstrate that the hair system could be employed as a technique to generate not only complex surfaces but also potential spatial arrangements. This notion of creation of space is achieved by displacing or disturbing field conditions with various geometrical objects defining various boundary conditions as a result.

The degree of densification and the global disturbance of the field are tested with soft and hard geometrical colliders. The result is different spatial boundary conditions; fuzzier and blurred in the case of the former example and crisper and defined in the latter.

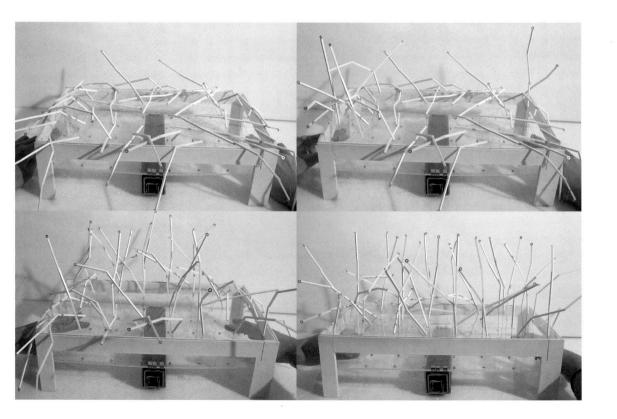

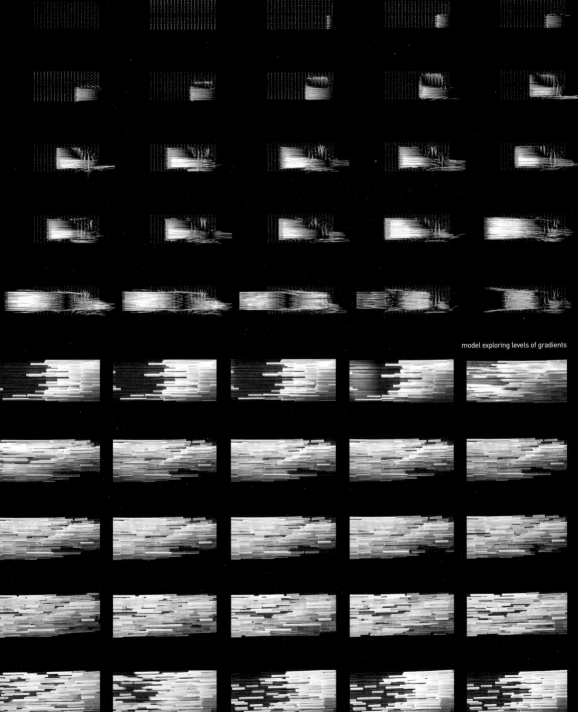

model exploring levels of gradients

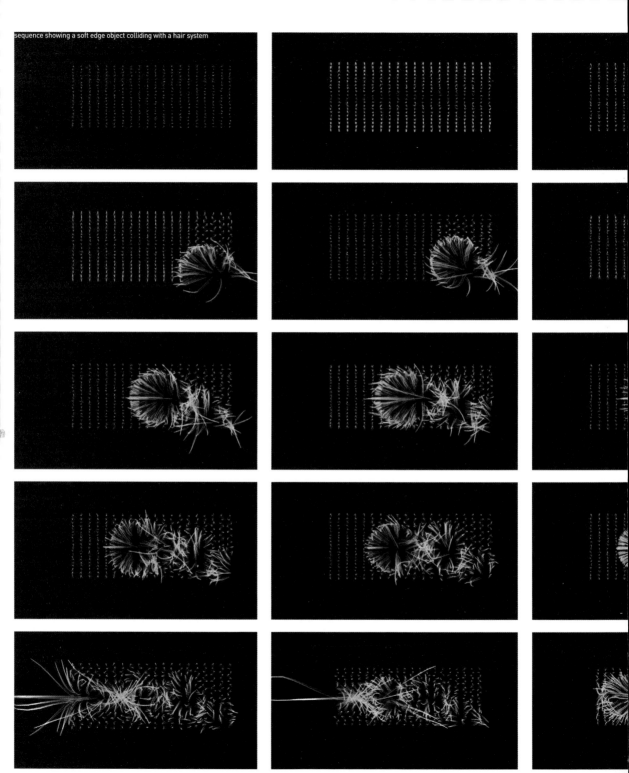

sequence showing a soft edge object colliding with a hair system

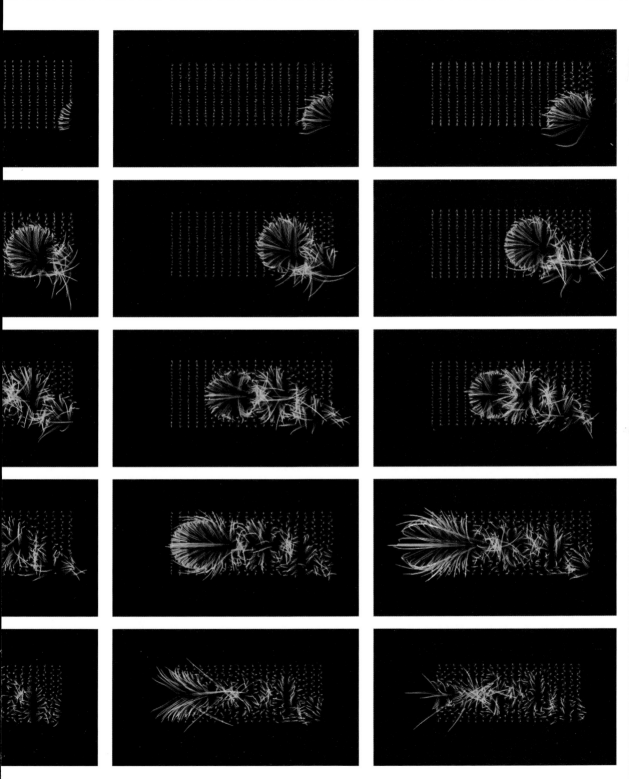

CURLS AND FREQUENCIES

In the following diagrams, the performance of the hair system was tested in order to produce various boundary conditions. Here the setups are made by either a single segmented hair or arrays of hairs subjected to varying curl degrees and frequency, as well as stiffness, mass and repulsion parameters.

Both setups have proven the capacity of the hair engine to create surfaces and volumes either by an arraying process or by a simpler way of bending and curling. These experiments demonstrate that the hair system was able to generate complex geometries emerging from fairly rational diagram setups. The degree of complexity of the resulting geometries doesn't appear directly proportional to the degree and frequency of the curls.

configuration of various hair systems with the same setup and different parameters

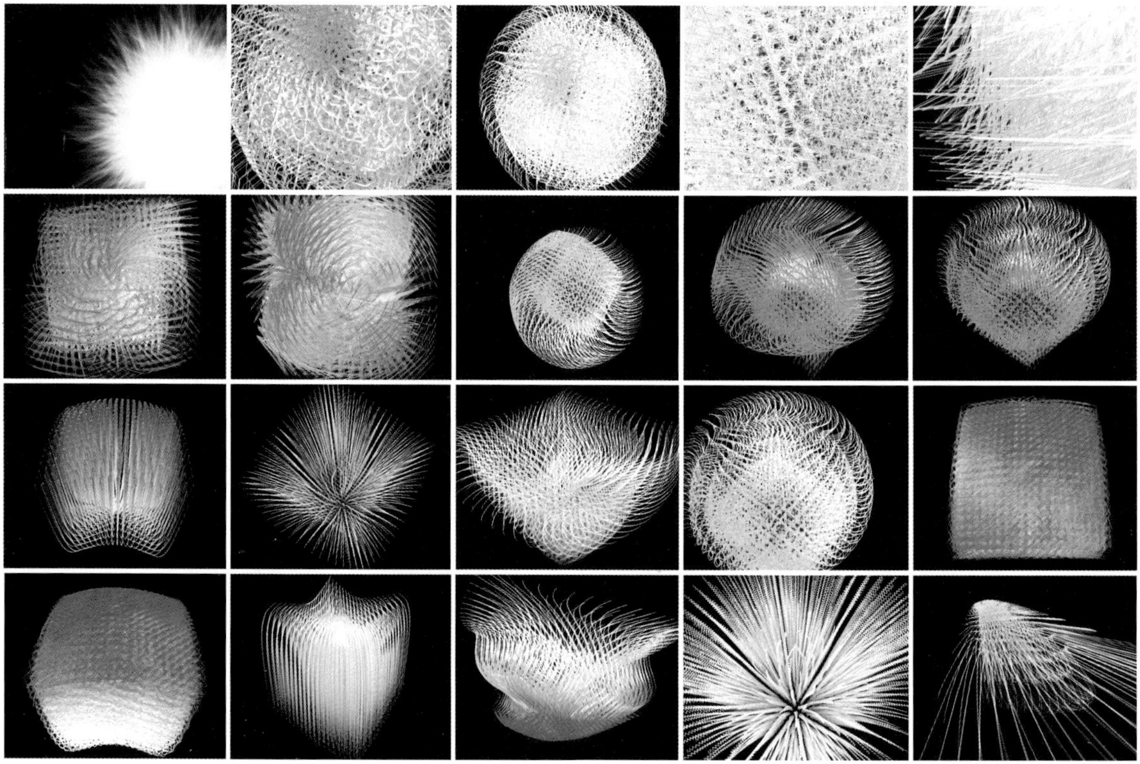

WORKING PATTERNS

In this series of diagrams, the self-organizing behaviour of the hair system is analyzed in order to evaluate its potential as an organizational tool and dynamic patterns generator. By manipulating parameters such as static cling, number of colliding neighbours, length flexibility and gravity over a certain time span, the resulting patterns range from a Miesian grid to complex fields of random lines.

These parameters driving the system are translated as literally as possible into different programmatic scenarios; the static cling and the number of colliding neighbours are read as potential degrees of flexibility and connectivity found in the new forms of workplaces and the collaborative environment. The higher the number of colliding neighbours, the more open the plan pattern is, and the higher the gravity and length flexibility, the more cell structured the plan develops into.

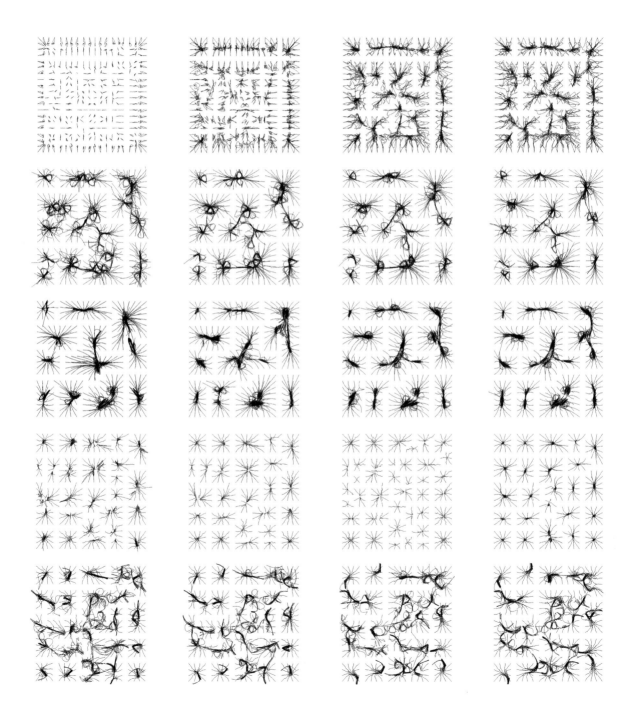

OPTIMISED PATH

Around the beginning of the 1990s, Frei Otto and his team at the Institute for Lightweight Structures studied what they called "optimized path system", analogous to the chain modelling technique that Gaudi used to design the Sagrada Familia. Both experimented with material systems for calculating form.

Each of these material experiments was devised so that a certain shape, pattern or form would result through numerous internal interactions. Most of the machines consisted of materials that can process forces by transformation. Otto's wool-thread machine was used to calculate the shapes of city patterns and branching systems. These are similar vector systems that economize on the number of paths by merging, bifurcating and sharing geometry.

The wool-water technique is a line to surface technique in which the lines are in the form of wool-threads and set up in a pattern with a certain amount of over length. Once the whole system is dipped in water, the threads start to merge and holes adjacent to the crossing threads start to form. What actually happens is an economization of detouring, the organization and regrouping of the extras. When the system dries one sees an emergent, self-organized order in which the lines suddenly form a network instead of a grid. In some instances lines have stuck together to form a thick line next to large open spots, and sometimes a small scale web of thin lines develops into something more surface-like.

Similar performance of this material system was further investigated using digital hair simulation.
The behaviours of the wool-threads system were translated into dynamic parameters acting on the behaviour of the hair. These flexible hairlines bundle with their nearest neighbouring hairs according to various parameters, constraints and static forces. The system finally reaches a stable state after a series of iterations of the algorithm is performed.
All of these techniques are fully systematic, all features are formed simultaneously. The system is calculating everything, solid and void, at the same time, during the same process through thousands of iterations where each positioning is dependent on the formation of another. Order and form are ultimately produced.

The constructive lines act as flexible hairlines that meet up and merge into a certain form, into a complex inflexibility in a bottom up process. This means that these computing techniques either analogue or digital are used to calculate not only structural form but also a higher level of organizational form.

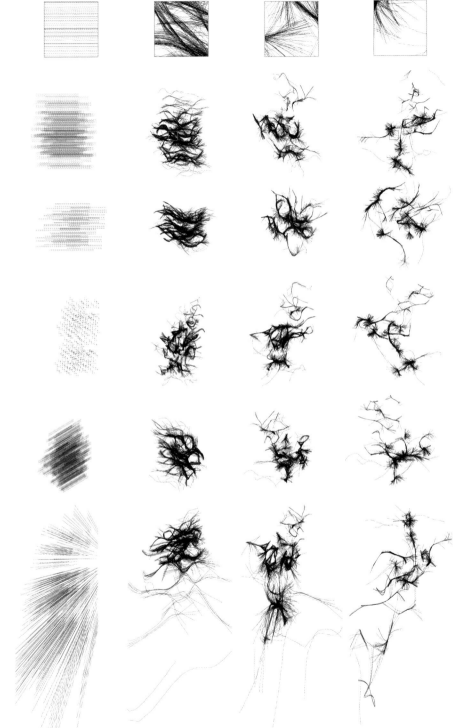

configuration of various hair systems with same parameters and different setups

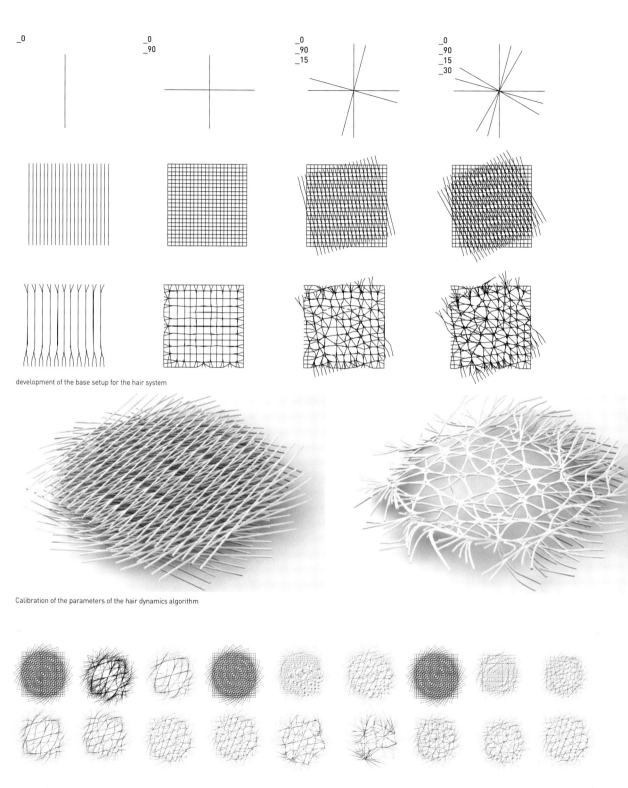

development of the base setup for the hair system

Calibration of the parameters of the hair dynamics algorithm

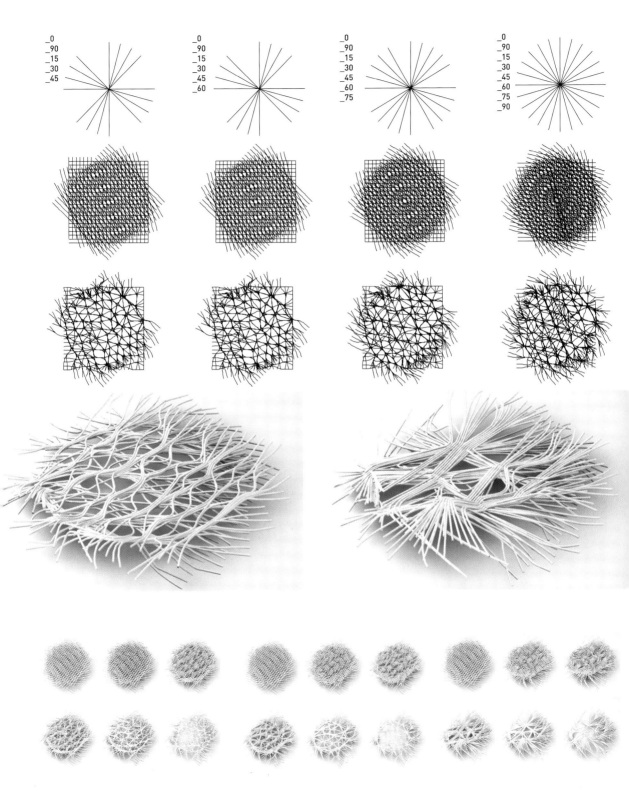

MATERIAL SYSTEM

The conclusions and rules extracted from the physical models were constantly feeding back into the research; they were brought forward into a digital format, enhancing the various digital diagramming and modelling techniques. As a result these laws became the basic structural principles responsible for the generation of the building form.

Going with the argument that structure is not around the space, but space is in and around the structure, the aim was to have the structural system perform along the complexities of the program, either by adapting to the changes or responding to the dynamics offered by different scenarios of the brief, finally resulting in the creation of boundaries for an effective programmed space.

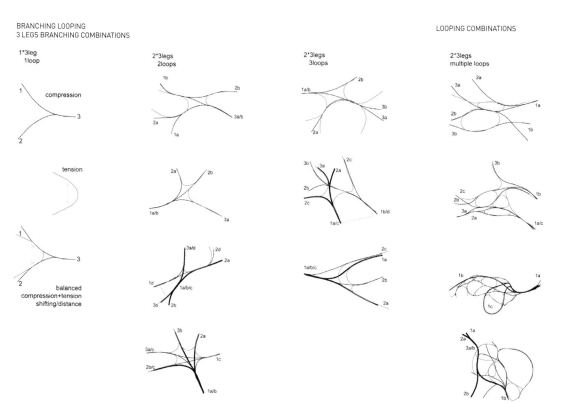

BRANCHING LOOPING
3 LEGS BRANCHING COMBINATIONS

LOOPING COMBINATIONS

Diagrams exploring the branching rules extracted from the piano wire study models

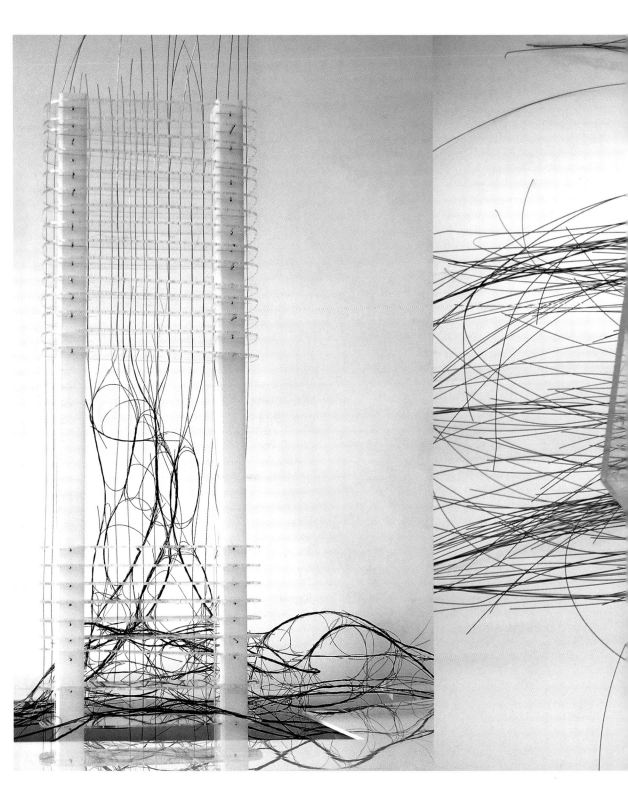

MORPHOGENESIS

2D / 3D SETUP

The starting point is a non-volumetric setup, where all the elements are interconnected in a network of hairlines attached to carefully distributed points and nodes. The hair dynamics algorithm is applied to this system of lines until the first two-dimensional pattern is formed. At this time the system becomes slightly stable, i.e. when the hairs have bundled with their specified nearby neighbours.

In order to extrude the system in the vertical dimension, additional attachment points or nodes are added in the three-dimensional constraining volume of the site marking the location of various programmatic lobbies. The algorithm is put into action again, this time resulting in a three dimensional line network.

What becomes most prominent in this dynamic system is that there is both an expression of rigidity and one of flexibility. It is a methodology that allows us to calculate the 'in between'. Form is at the edges, diagram in the middle. Spatially, it results in a porous bone-like structure, in which the surface shell is more dense and solid than the inside. It is not a Cartesian option but more an actual fuzzy material state of 'in between' that is internalized and functioning.

C00: corner node
M00: mid node
⬯ : transit users
⬭ : users of site

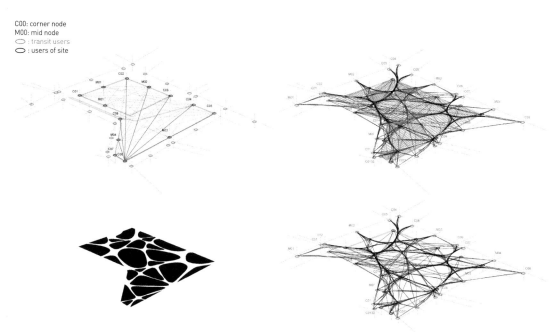

Diagrams showing the application of the hair system algorithm on the project's site and the resulting two-dimensional circulation patterns and programmatic zones

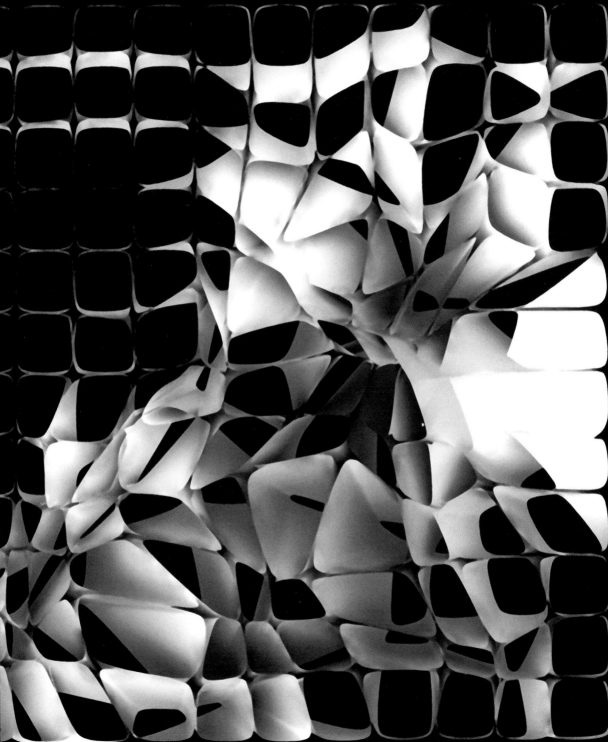

SITE EDGE CONDITIONS
3D HAIR SITE SETUP

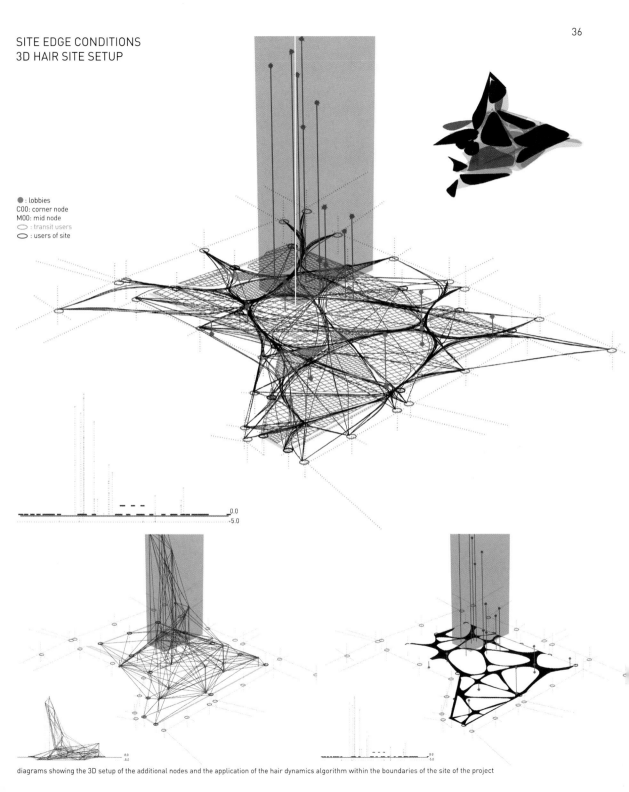

● : lobbies
C00: corner node
M00: mid node
⬭ : transit users
⬭ : users of site

diagrams showing the 3D setup of the additional nodes and the application of the hair dynamics algorithm within the boundaries of the site of the project

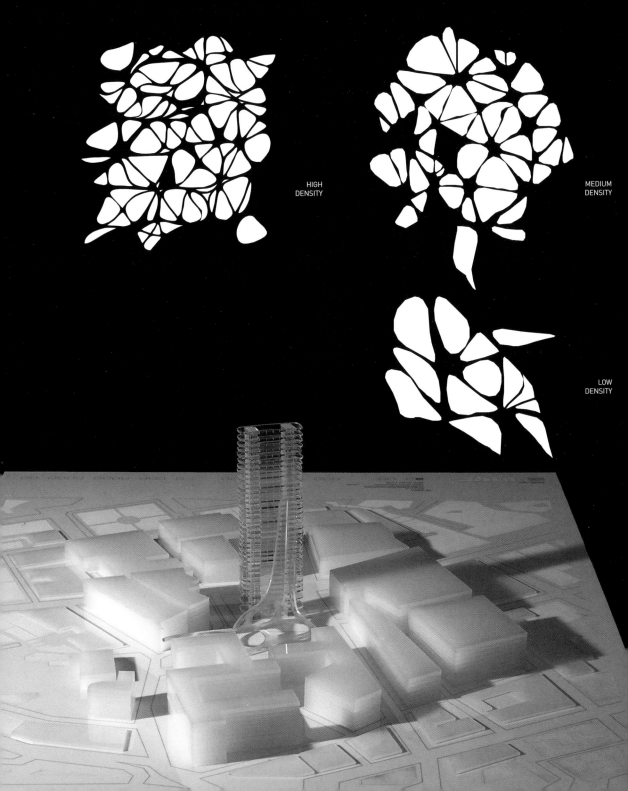

HIGH
DENSITY

MEDIUM
DENSITY

LOW
DENSITY

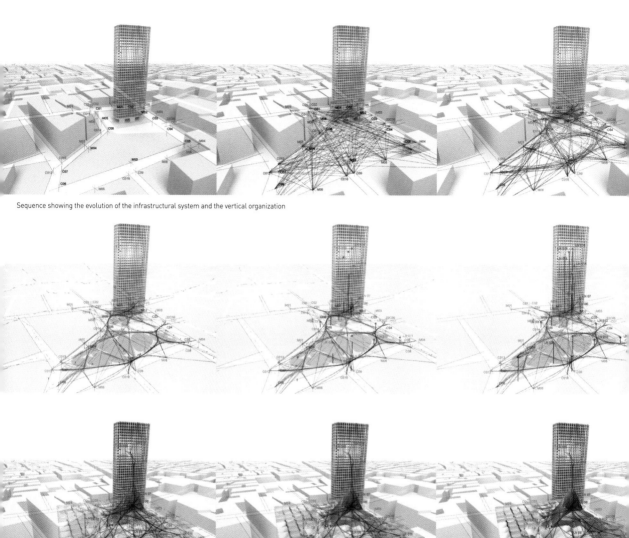

Sequence showing the evolution of the infrastructural system and the vertical organization

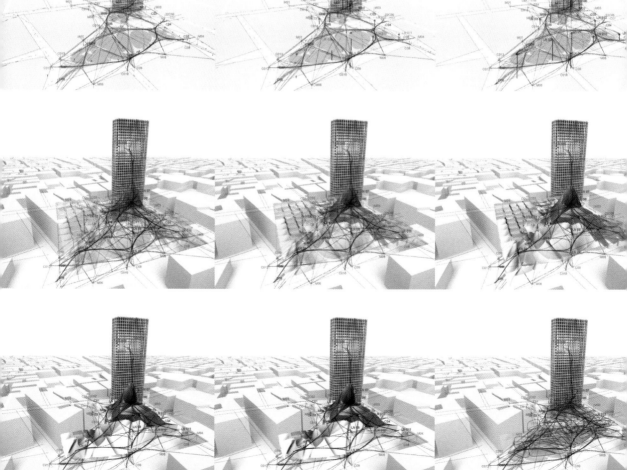

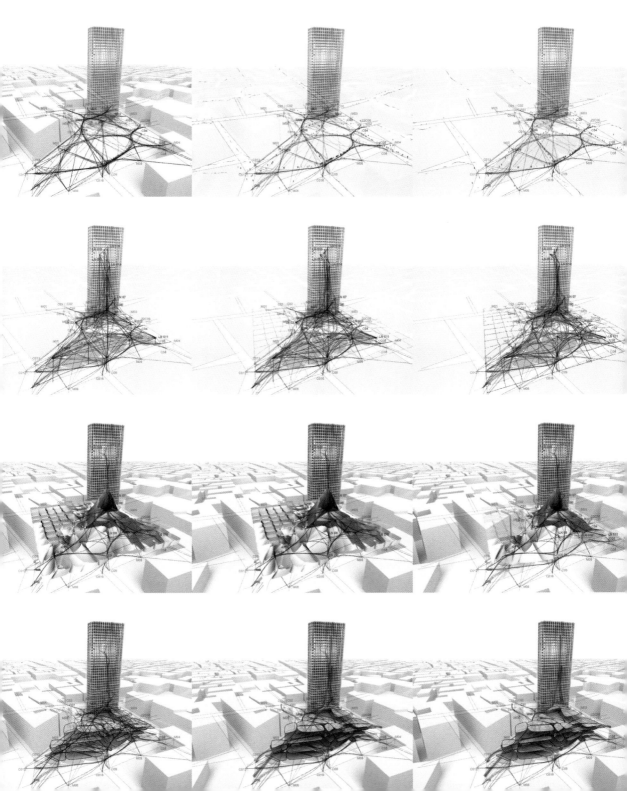

CIRCULATION

After numerous iterations; the network of hair lines bundles together and reaches a stable state. As a result a path is generated; it clearly corresponds to the infrastructural path on the project. The post-production of that diagram aimed to actualize the path system and assign it a scale. Therefore various design decisions were made in order to allocate stairs, ramps, escalators entrances and vertical shafts. Finally, this path was divided in different circulation segments after various modifications were made to adjust the slopes and lengths of these building systems and get them to the right standards.

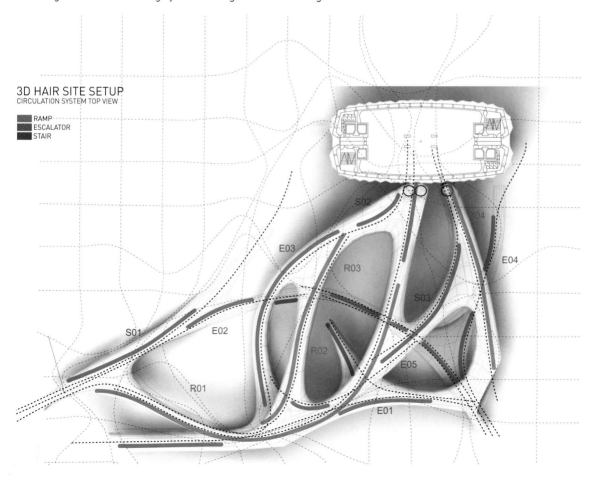

3D HAIR SITE SETUP
CIRCULATION SYSTEM TOP VIEW

RAMP
ESCALATOR
STAIR

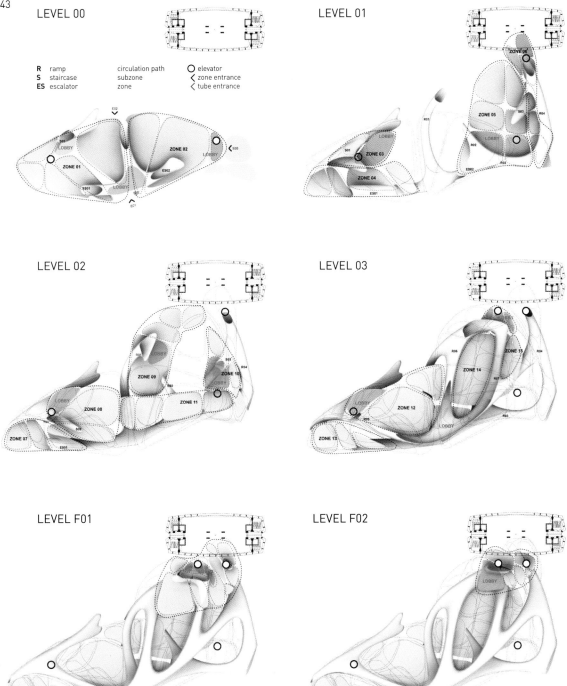

LEVEL 00

R   ramp
S   staircase
ES escalator

circulation path
subzone
zone

○ elevator
‹ zone entrance
‹ tube entrance

LEVEL 01

LEVEL 02

LEVEL 03

LEVEL F01

LEVEL F02

Diagrams showing the distribution of the program around the main circulation arteries on the Urban Lobby

PROGRAM ORGANIZATION

The bottom up process developed in this main agenda combined research and experimentation on a dynamic system involving digital hair simulation. Several attempts using this hair diagram tool were made to generate a formal language with structural logic that could potentially become a space frame for various programmatic activities.

Various techniques were therefore elaborated to systematise this digital process in order to test it at a larger scale as an organizational tool for the program distribution of the project, and at a smaller scale, as a tectonic diagram responsible for the structural logic of the project, fitting all its infrastructural systems and subsystems together in an elegant assembly.

The preliminary level of intervention for this project starts with the extension of the 10 by 10 meter grid of the existing structure of the Center Point building over the entire site of the project. Using the hair diagram setups and parameters elaborated earlier, the grid is deformed creating a series of grids that reorganize the spaces in a more dynamic and differentiated pattern. These grids generate interconnected floor plates patterns and various nested zones that will host the programmatic functions for the Urban Lobby.

The investigation of grids and deformation of lattices opened a new chapter in MRGD's research agenda. Being one of the essential elements in parametric software, grids and surface grids constitute the environment in which components could be sited. Therefore, the techniques for manipulating and distorting these grids become as crucial as the design of the components themselves.

The following diagrams illustrate the morphogenesis of the Urban Lobby as well as its internal organization. It begins with the dynamic hair system, which becomes not only the circulation and infrastructural diagram for the project, but also the grounds for the deformation of the grids as explained earlier. As a result, the deformed spatial components nest among each other and, once sliced horizontally according to the circulation path, they allocate the geometry and positioning of the floors across the entire building. This emerging vertical pattern of the floor plates stands out against the layered organization of the existing model of Center Point.

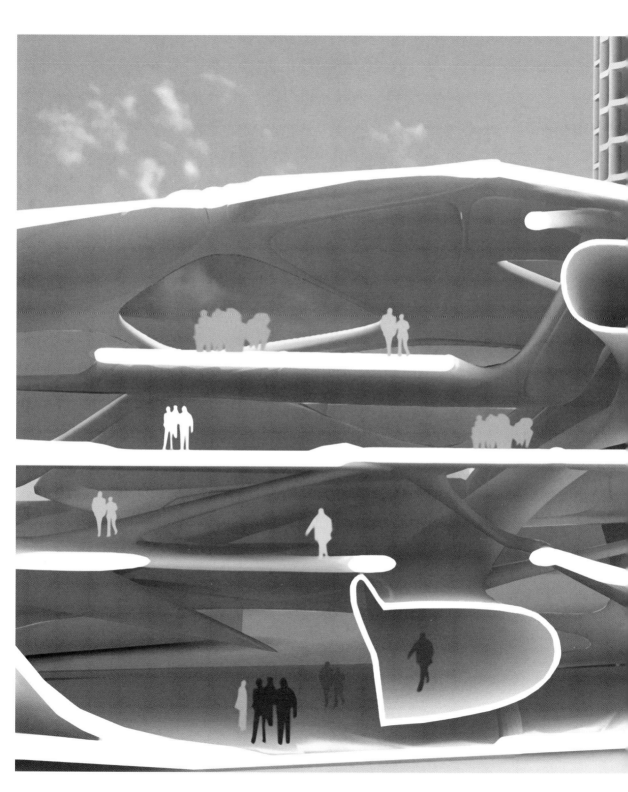

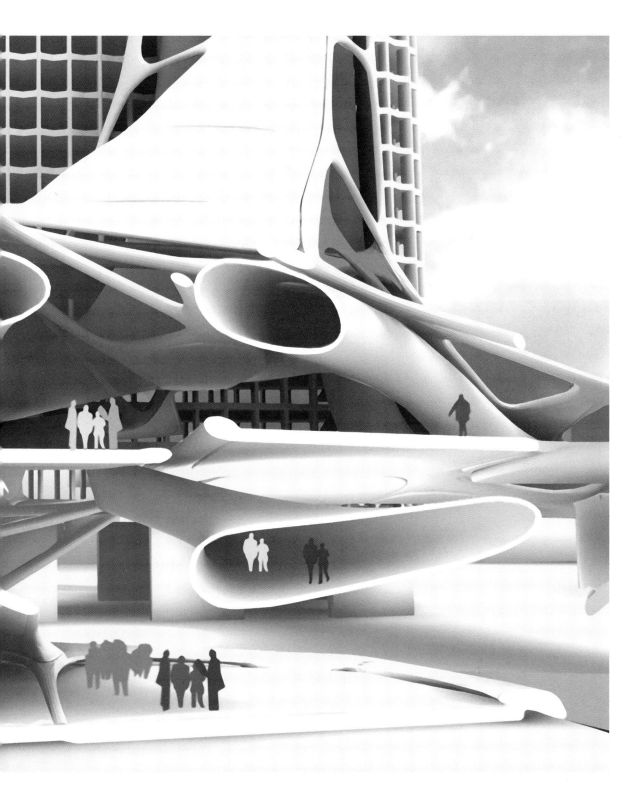

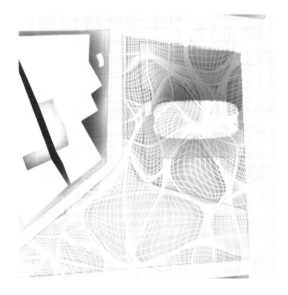
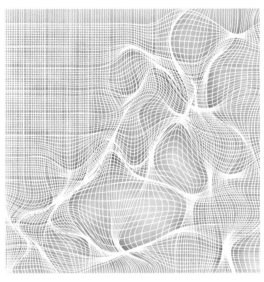

Series of deformed grids and surface grids subject to the hair dynamics forces

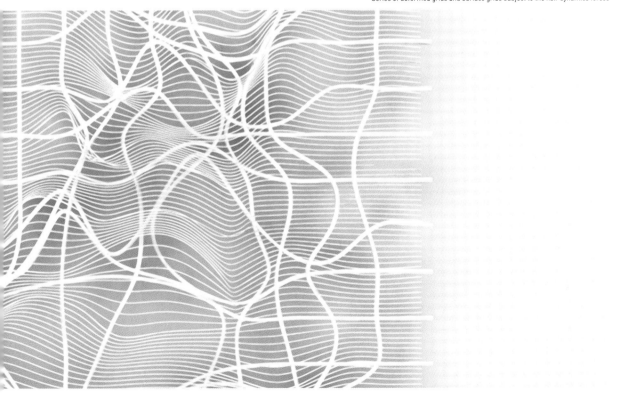

3D HAIR SETUP

2D HAIR SETUP

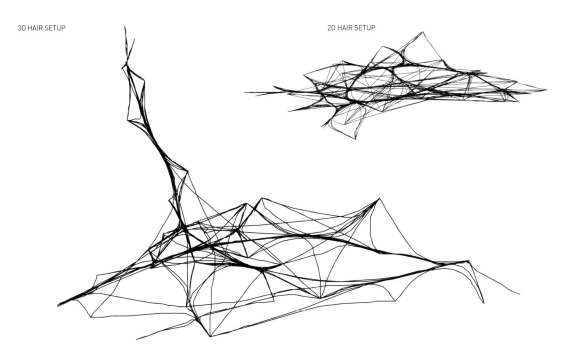

SITE SETUP 2D COMPONENT / GROUND PATTERN

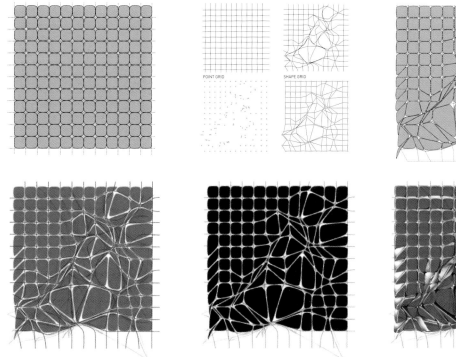

POINT GRID

SHAPE GRID

SITE SETUP 2D COMPONENT / GROUND PATTERN

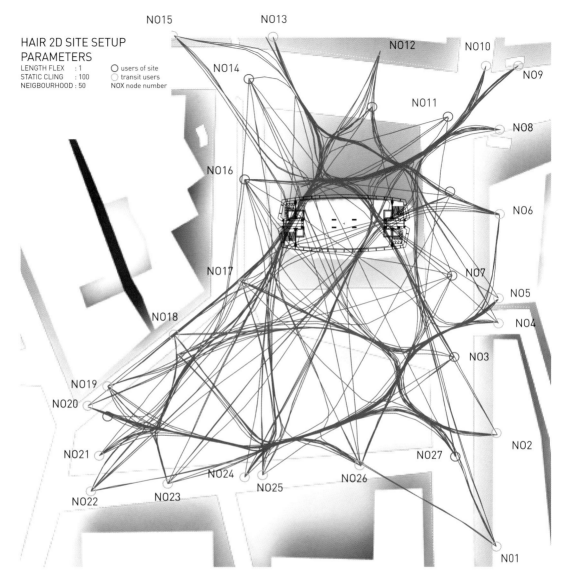

HAIR 2D SITE SETUP
PARAMETERS

LENGTH FLEX : 1
STATIC CLING : 100
NEIGBOURHOOD : 50

○ users of site
◐ transit users
NOX node number

NO15 NO13 NO12 NO10 NO09 NO14 NO11 NO08 NO16 NO06 NO17 NO07 NO05 NO04 NO18 NO03 NO19 NO20 NO02 NO21 NO27 NO24 NO26 NO22 NO23 NO25 NO01

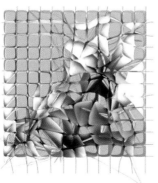

SITE GC GRID SETUP
PARAMETERS

CENTERPOINT STRUCTURAL GRID: 10M/10M
CENTERPOINT FACADE GRID: 2.5M/2.5M

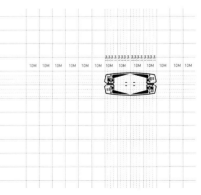

10M 10M 10M 10M 10M 10M 10M 10M 10M 10M 10M 10M 10M 10M

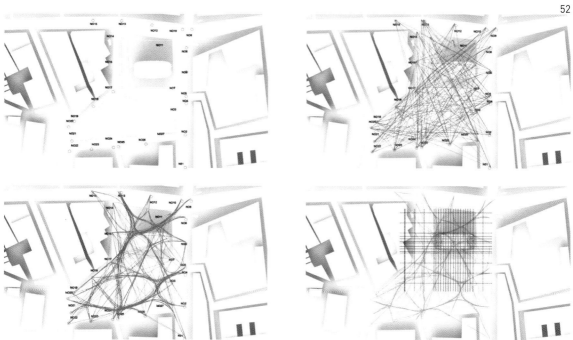

Series of diagrams explaining the transformation of the linear structural grid of the existing fabric into the non linear grid of the proposed project

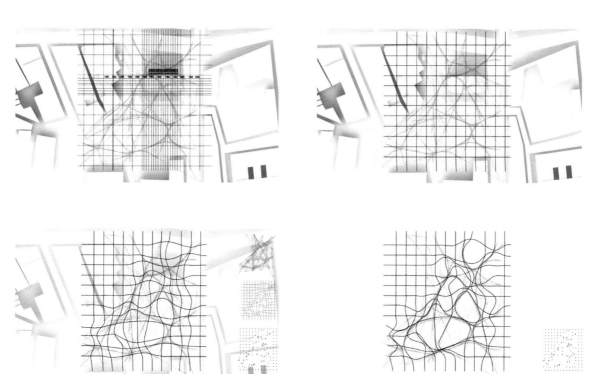

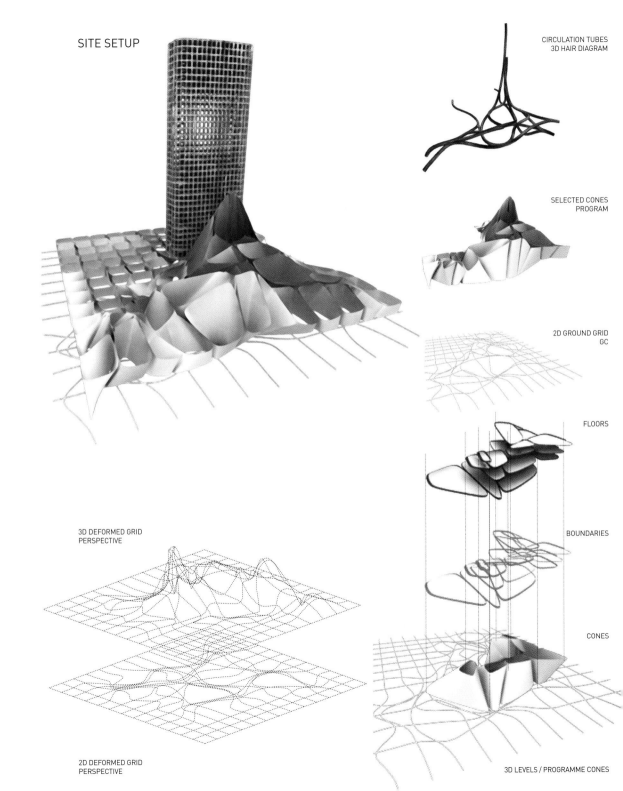

SITE SETUP

CIRCULATION TUBES
3D HAIR DIAGRAM

SELECTED CONES
PROGRAM

2D GROUND GRID
GC

FLOORS

BOUNDARIES

CONES

3D DEFORMED GRID
PERSPECTIVE

2D DEFORMED GRID
PERSPECTIVE

3D LEVELS / PROGRAMME CONES

TECTONICS

Through various digital experiments with the hair system, logics for structural capabilities are sieved out; rules are extracted regarding the fillet angles and radii at the branching intersections, and the thicknesses related to the length of the branches.

Based on these rules, the component created in Generative Components intends to mimic the behaviour of the hair bundles at the intersection of multiple branches. This joint is realised as an intersection of solid legs that are capable of stretching and adapting their dimensions. Generative Components is employed to create interdependencies between the legs of the component and build an interactive continuity between several joints to generate a structural three dimensional lattice that will become a proposal for the structural integrity of the project.

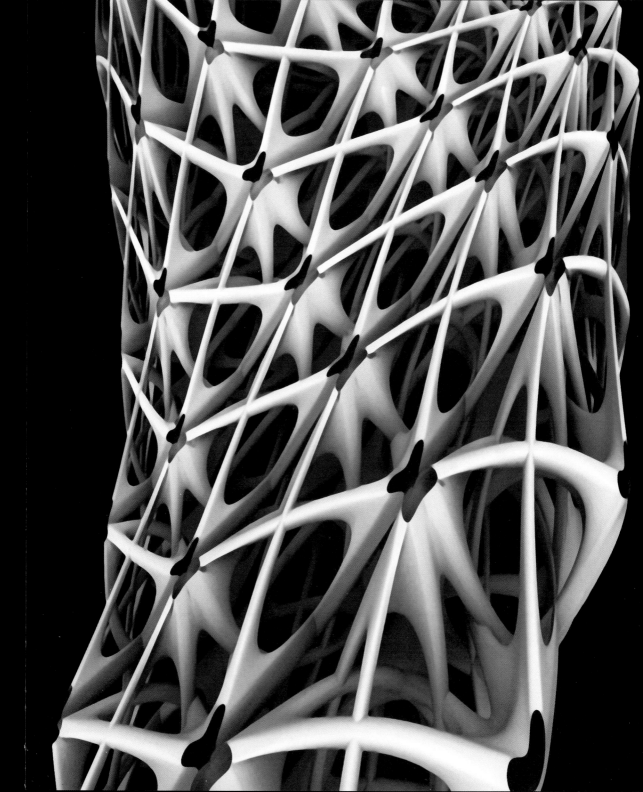

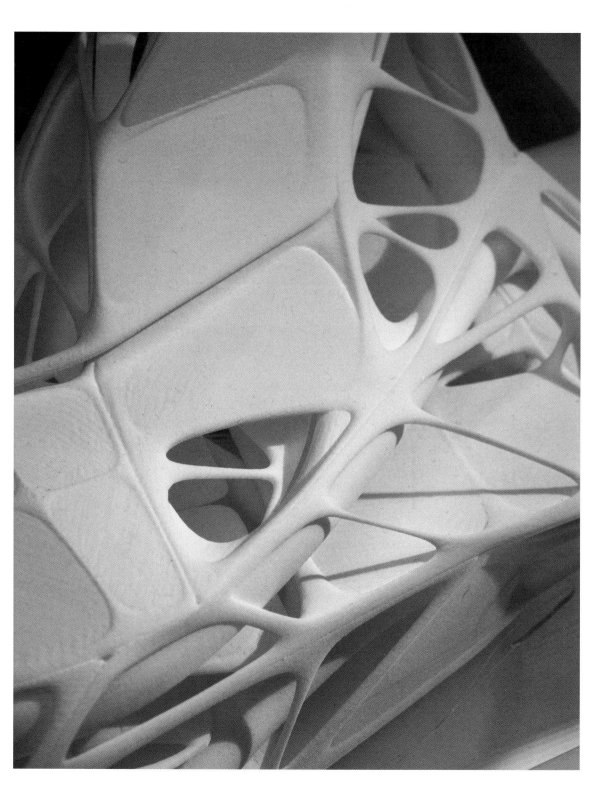

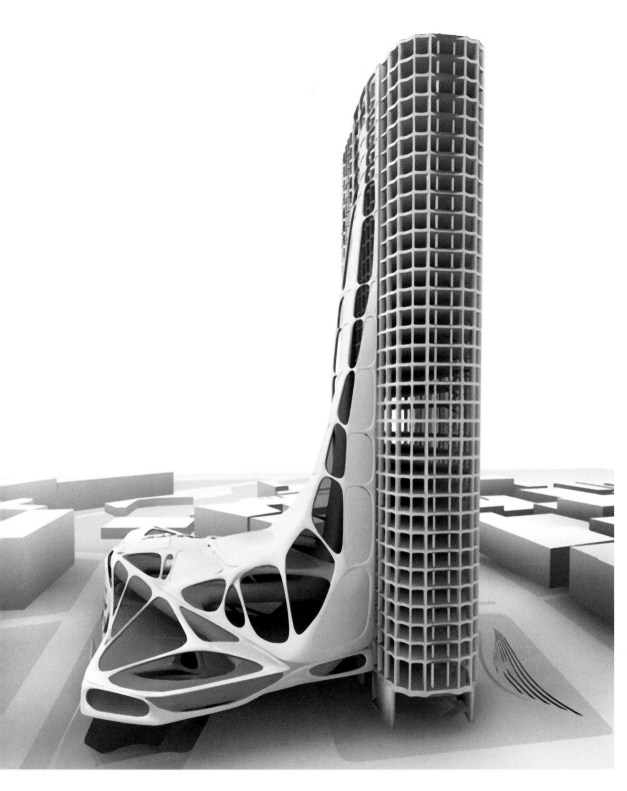

LATTICE

Generative Components was used to design the components and lattices as well as the myriad variations to meet precisely the needs for structural and organizational differentiation. Interrelations established between components proliferate them, seamlessly achieving a differential distribution of material with flawless continuity.

Various embedded digital features are then explored to test different component spreading modes. The components are spread over different surfaces and point grids controlled by law curves that provide control over the various possible deformations of the surfaces.

The aim of all these experiments is to achieve continuity between the existing structural lattice of Center Point and the structural envelope of the Urban Lobby proposal. The control of the deformations of the grids and consequently the variations of the proliferated components is essential not only to aesthetically differentiate the structural building envelope, but also to control the level of local porosity in certain zones of the project.

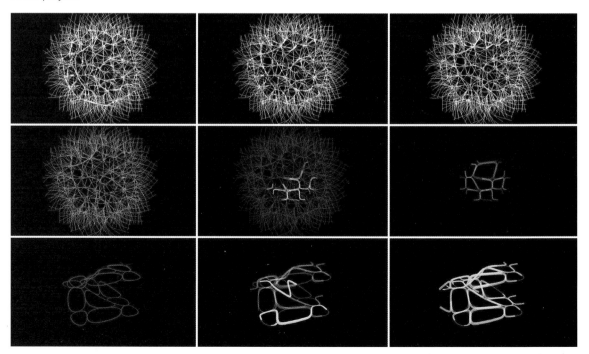

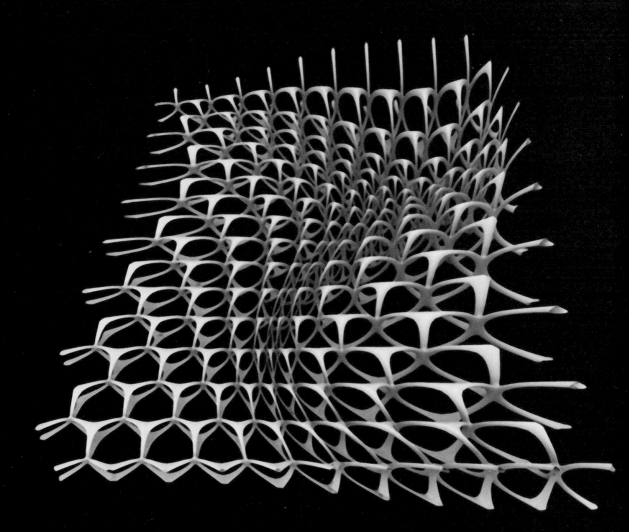

Speculative Studies of Surface deformation controlled by law curves in Generative Components

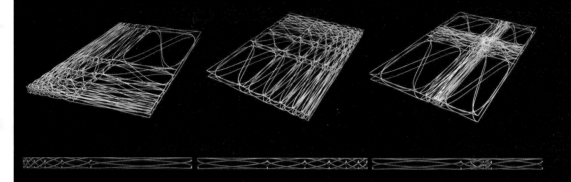

Construction of four legged joints dependent on various structural rules and constraints setup in Generative Components

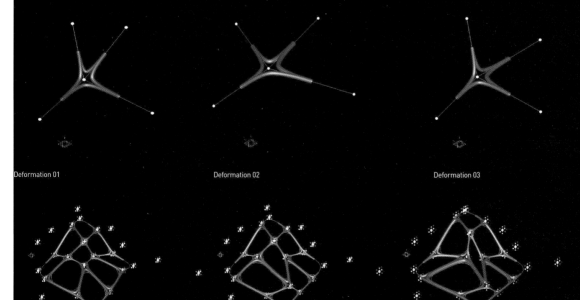

Deformation 01   Deformation 02   Deformation 03

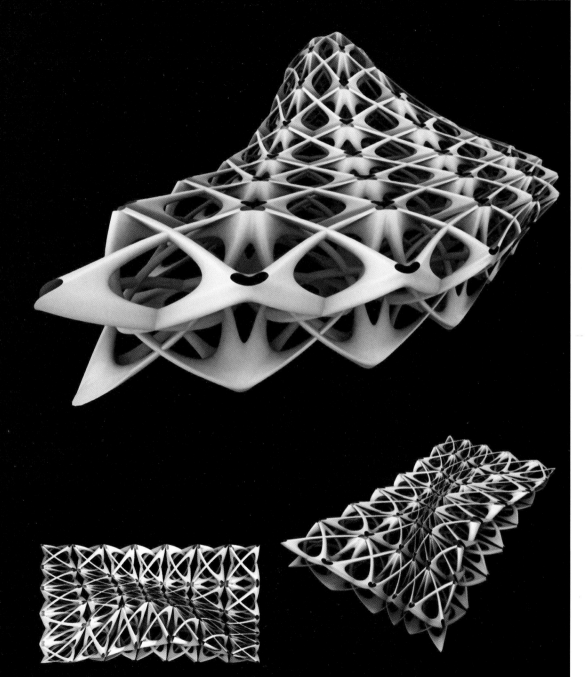

DIGITAL FABRICATION

Generating new forms guides the imagination towards buildings that reflect rather than contradict real design constraints. Digital design tools are therefore used not only to generate new organic forms but also direct towards efficient forms that can be built effectively.

The framework here was used to build evaluative tools that can address key issues of building performance. The aim of the prototype models was to translate the generated component behaviors into physical production. The joint components were isolated from the lattice and sent through laser cutting, CNC milling, molding and casting processes to achieve the correct leg thicknesses and fillet angles.

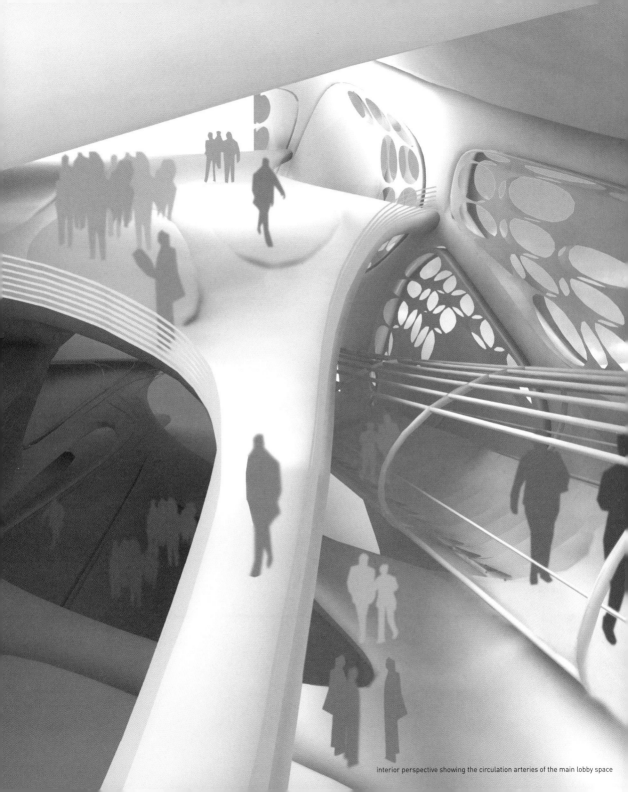

interior perspective showing the circulation arteries of the main lobby space

prototype of structural bundling

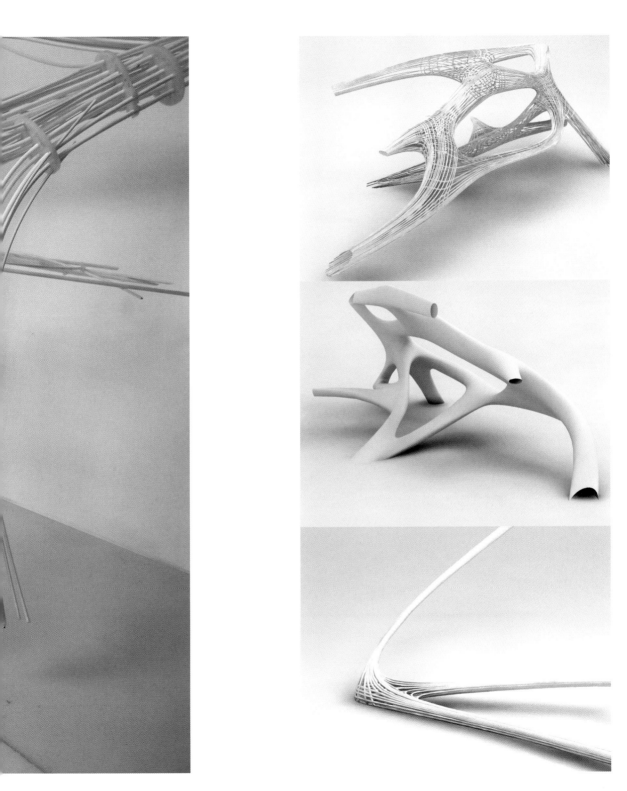

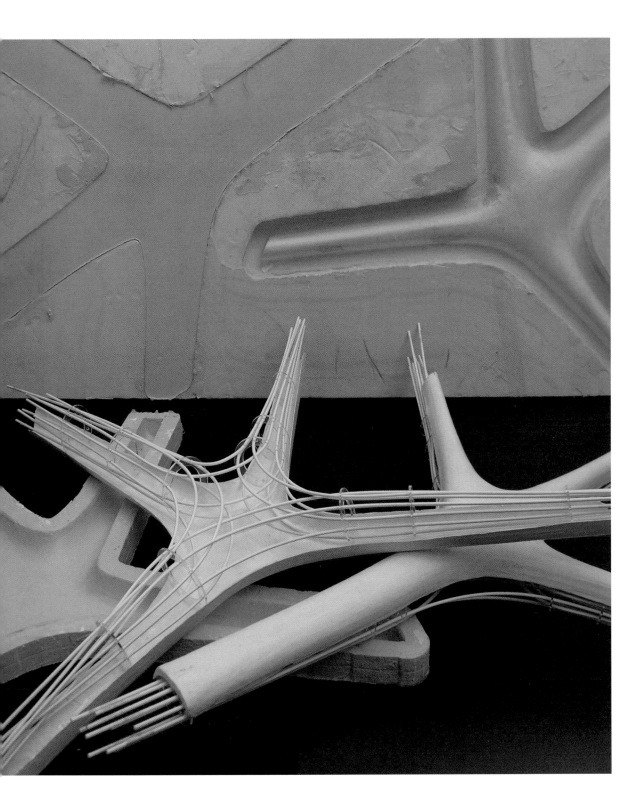

PROTOTYPE

MRGD constantly rethought the potential of non conventional and non linear structures. It resorted to a methodological solution using digital computational techniques adding to Frei Otto's analogue experiments. Throughout the year it created and customized its own techniques and tools aiming to design complex structures which are fully based on variability. Through a very precise set of operations these tools allow the creation of systems that are structurally in between beams and columns, architecturally in between roof and floor, and that are programmatically in between determined and indetermined.

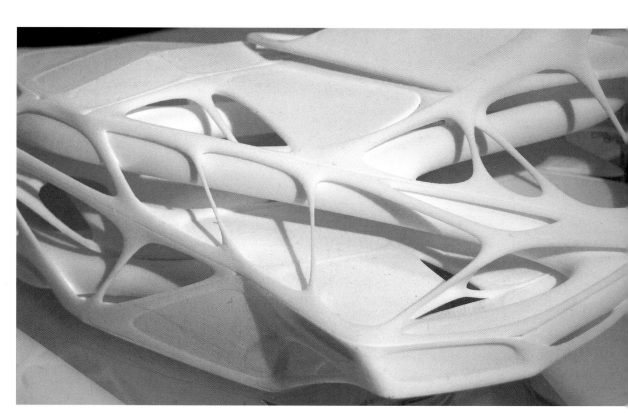

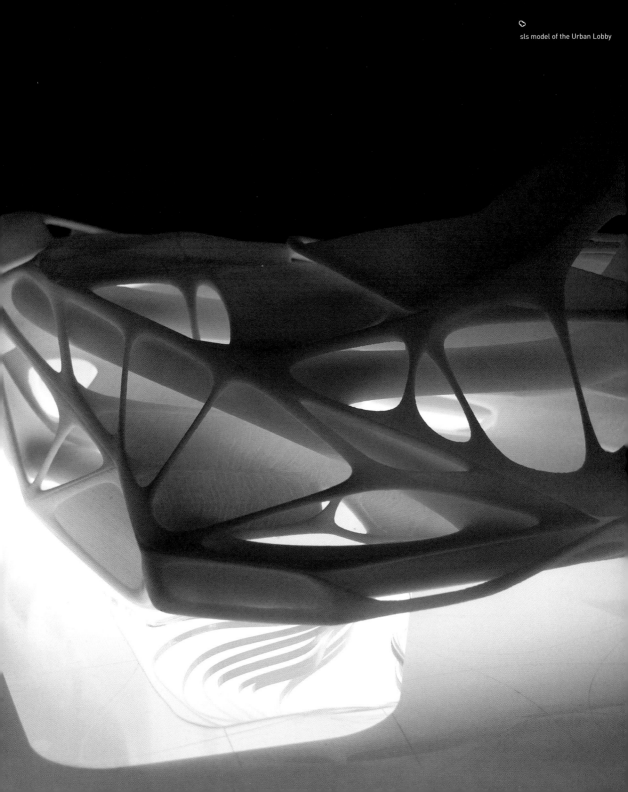

CONCLUSION

The intention of the project is not a simple scaling up of a material system to the level of real structural components consisting of bundles of tubes of certain sizes. Instead it is a sophisticated layered project with multiple systems and subsystems interacting in an organic way.

The form builds up with a circulation logic based on the hair system's algorithm, followed by a post-production phase highlighting the primary arteries which become circulation paths and secondary lines which become structural spines. The form is complemented by an additional skinning system highly driven into the primary. The process folds back and the work shifts to the mode of architectural detailing, in which meaning is given to the primary lattice-style tubes, producing them as ramps and staircases and opening them to create polycentric lobby spaces with multiple entrances and connections. This is when elegance comes to fall in a project so absorbed in the architectural articulation of space and form making.

This brings up the discussion of two complementary yet different concepts: beauty vs. elegance. Technique comes to play its major role to transform what is considered 'not beautiful' to 'beautiful' as it does in the field of plastic surgery. Elegance is therefore achieved as a kind of problem solving process, an ability to articulate complexity, and multiple agendas into a resolution. It's an elaborated condition; whereas beauty is a lucky hit, elegance is a resolution of multiple agendas into complex articulated and resolved conditions. All the use of logics, continuities and algorithms, applied as for differentiation, were part of this step towards elegance.

This process becomes virtuosity when we creatively solve the interpolation and inter-articulation into the organic domain by methods that happen through evolution, trial and error and cross interpretation of systems all leading to production of elegance.

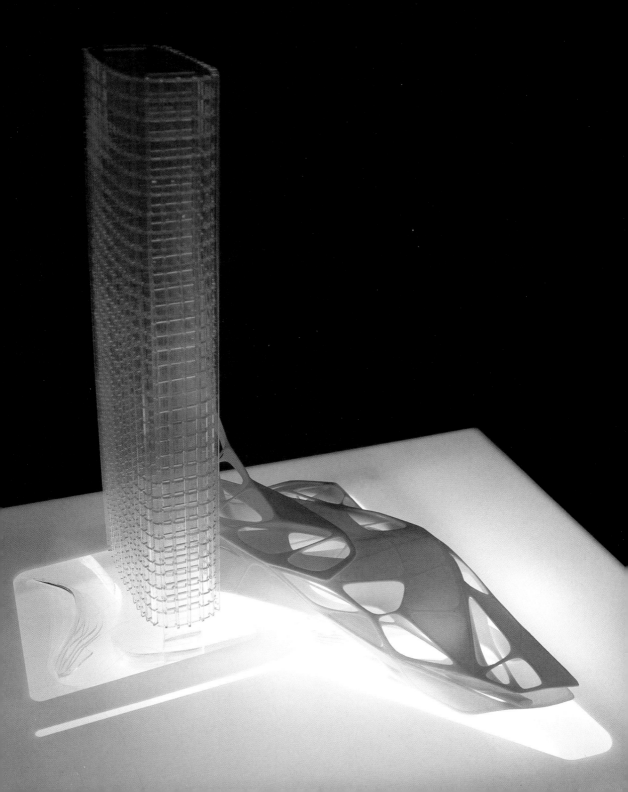

ACKNOWLEDGEMENTS

This is to thank all the people who collaborated with MRGD to make this book project happen. We also would like to express our appreciation to all the tutors and critics who kept us inspired and gave us constructive and useful advices. We hereby thank the following persons, and the many others who are not mentioned by name, for their effort:
Patrik Schumacher, Brett Steele, Theodore Spyropoulos, Vasili Stroumpakos, Tom Verebes, Florian Dubiel, Edgar Payan, Amit Gupta, Shajay Bhooshan, Yoshimasa Hagiwara, Nanatapon Junngurn, Andrea Johnson, Nick Puckett, Ali Rahim, Lars Spuybroek and Frei Otto.
And last but not least a very special acknowledgment to all our families and friends who supported us all along the way.

MRGD

MRGD is a design research collaboration of young architects; Melike Altinisik, Samer Chamoun and Daniel Widrig. Since it was founded in 2004, MRGD researches on various parametric design tools exploring in parallel the ideas of form finding, self organization and digital manufacturing. MRGD's thesis project, URBAN LOBBY was first presented at the Architectural Association in London. Their work has won several awards such as the FEIDAD Award 2006 and the Swiss Arts Award 2007 and was exhibited and published in London and around the world.

www.mrgd.co.uk/

Springer Architecture

RIEAeuropa Book Series

Lars Kordetzky
Sequences
Saw only the Moon
2001. 100 pages. Num. figures, mosty in col.
Softcover **EUR 23,–**
ISBN 978-3-211-83642-2

Mas Yendo
Ironic Diversion
2001. 104 pages. Numerous figures in col.
Softcover **EUR 26,–**
ISBN 978-3-211-83492-3

Margot K. Krasojevic
Spatial Pathology-Floating Realities
2007. 111 pages. Numerous figures.
Softcover **EUR 24,95**
ISBN 978-3-211-71533-8

RIEAeuropa Concepts Series

Lebbeus Woods
Earthquake!
A Post-Biblical View
2001. 52 pages. Numerous figures.
Softcover **EUR 14,75**
ISBN 978-3-211-83643-9

L. Woods, G. Lafranchi (eds.)
Gr(o)und
Workshop 2002
2003. 56 pages. Numerous figures.
Softcover **EUR 16,–**
ISBN 978-3-211-00642-9

L. Woods, G. Lafranchi (eds.)
Histaormina
Workshop 2001
2002. 56 pages. 62 figures.
Softcover **EUR 16,–**
ISBN 978-3-211-83794-8

G. Lafranchi, D. Egger
Prisoners of Museum
2001. 67 pages. Numerous figures.
Softcover **EUR 14,75**
ISBN 978-3-211-83644-6

Sotirios Kotoulas
Space Out
2005. 103 pages. Numerous figures.
Softcover **EUR 19,–**
ISBN 978-3-211-24488-3

Lars Kordetzky
Transient Sedimentation
2006. 72 pages. Numerous figures.
Softcover **EUR 24,–**
ISBN 978-3-211-32193-5

N. Jackowski, R. O. C. de Ostos
The Hanging Cemetery of Baghdad
2007. 71 pages. Numerous figures.
Softcover **EUR 24,95**
ISBN 978-3-211-48872-0

 SpringerWienNewYork

P. O. Box 89, Sachsenplatz 4–6, 1201 Vienna, Austria, Fax +43.1.330 24 26, books@springer.at, **springer.at**
Birkhäuser c/o SDC, Haberstraße 7, 69126 Heidelberg, Germany, Fax: +49.6221.345-4229, SDC-bookorder@springer.com
P. O. Box 2485, Secaucus, NJ 07096-2485, USA, Fax +1.201.348-4505, service@springer.com, springeronline.com. All errors and omissions excepted.